7x 12/08   4 - 03-

D0398791

PRESIDENTS

JAMES
MADISON

A MyReportLinks.com Book

Neil D. Bramwell

MyReportLinks.com Books

an imprint of

 Enslow Publishers, Inc.

Box 398, 40 Industrial Road
Berkeley Heights, NJ 07922
USA

MyReportLinks.com Books, an imprint of Enslow Publishers, Inc. MyReportLinks is a trademark of Enslow Publishers, Inc.

Library of Congress Cataloging-in-Publication Data

Bramwell, Neil D., 1932–
    James Madison / Neil D. Bramwell.
       p. cm. — (Presidents)
Summary: A biography of the fourth president of the United States, who helped ensure ratification of the Constitution and the Bill of Rights. Includes Internet links to Web sites, source documents, and photographs related to James Madison.
Includes bibliographical references and index.
   ISBN 0-7660-5129-3
   1. Madison, James, 1751–1836—Juvenile literature. 2. Presidents—United States—Biography—Juvenile literature. [1. Madison, James, 1751-1836. 2. Presidents.] I. Title. II. Series.
E342.B68 2003
973.5'1'092--dc21

                            2002014849

Printed in the United States of America

10 9 8 7 6 5 4 3 2 1

To Our Readers:
Through the purchase of this book, you and your library gain access to the Report Links that specifically back up this book.
The Publisher will provide access to the Report Links that back up this book and will keep these Report Links up to date on www.myreportlinks.com for three years from the book's first publication date.
We have done our best to make sure all Internet addresses in this book were active and appropriate when we went to press. However, the author and the Publisher have no control over, and assume no liability for, the material available on those Internet sites or on other Web sites they may link to.
The usage of the MyReportLinks.com Books Web site is subject to the terms and conditions stated on the Usage Policy Statement on www.myreportlinks.com.
In the future, a password may be required to access the Report Links that back up this book. The password is found on the bottom of page 4 of this book.
Any comments or suggestions can be sent by e-mail to comments@myreportlinks.com or to the address on the back cover.

Photo Credits: © Corel Corporation, pp. 1 (background), 3; Department of the Interior, pp. 32, 37; Founding Fathers.info, p. 19; Howard Chandler Christy, p. 17; James Madison's Montpelier, p. 13; Library of Congress, pp. 1, (portrait), 30, 34, 40, 42; Louisiana Department of State and Louisiana's Old State Capitol, p. 28; MyReportLinks.com Books, p. 4; National Archives, pp. 25, 38, 39; Painting by Allyn Cox, p. 11; Painting by John Trumball, p. 21; The White House, p. 23.

Cover Photo: Hulton Archive by Getty Images

Contents

MyReportLinks.com Books
Great Books, Great Links, Great for Research!

MyReportLinks.com Books present the information you need to learn about your report subject. In addition, they show you where to go on the Internet for more information. The pre-evaluated Report Links that back up this book are kept up to date on **www.myreportlinks.com**. With the purchase of a MyReportLinks.com Books title, you and your library gain access to the Report Links that specifically back up that book. The Report Links save hours of research time and link to dozens—even hundreds—of Web sites, source documents, and photos related to your report topic.

Please see "To Our Readers" on the Copyright page for important information about this book, the MyReportLinks.com Books Web site, and the Report Links that back up this book.

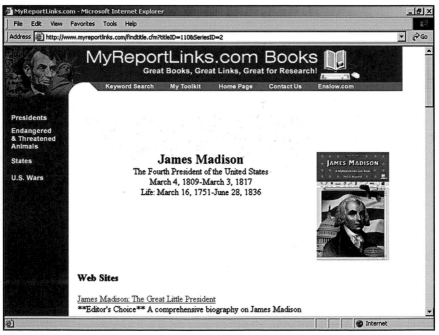

Access:

The Publisher will provide access to the Report Links that back up this book and will try to keep these Report Links up to date on our Web site for three years from the book's first publication date. Please enter **PMA5315** if asked for a password.

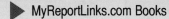
Report Links

 The Internet sites described below can be accessed at
http://www.myreportlinks.com

▶**James Madison: The Great Little President**
*EDITOR'S CHOICE

This comprehensive Web site provides detailed information about
President James Madison. Here you will learn about his early life,
presidential campaigns, domestic and foreign affairs, the first lady, and
his legacy. You will also find images, quotes, and additional resources.

Link to this Internet site from http://www.myreportlinks.com

▶**The American President: The Balance of Power**
*EDITOR'S CHOICE

The American President Web site profiles four presidents who
tilted the balance of power. Here you will learn how James Madison,
one of the four presidents profiled, felt about the balance of power
in government.

Link to this Internet site from http://www.myreportlinks.com

▶**Presidents of the United States: James Madison**
*EDITOR'S CHOICE

The POTUS Web site provides facts and figures on James Madison.
Here you will find election results, cabinet appointments, information
about Madison's family, and important events in his administration.

Link to this Internet site from http://www.myreportlinks.com

▶**James Monroe Sought Advice from Thomas Jefferson**
*EDITOR'S CHOICE

America's Story from America's Library, a Library of Congress Web site,
tells the story of Monroe seeking advice from Jefferson with regards to
foreign affairs.

Link to this Internet site from http://www.myreportlinks.com

▶**The Avalon Project: The Papers of James Madison**
*EDITOR'S CHOICE

In addition to James Madison's two inaugural addresses, here you will
also find the complete text of the Virginia Resolution and Madison's
notes on the debates of the 1787 Federal Convention.

Link to this Internet site from http://www.myreportlinks.com

▶**The James Madison Center**
*EDITOR'S CHOICE

The James Madison Center provides a wealth of information about
Madison's family, legacy, and home.

Link to this Internet site from http://www.myreportlinks.com

The Internet sites described below can be accessed at
http://www.myreportlinks.com

▶**The American Presidency: Bill of Rights**
This Web site describes the history of the Bill of Rights and provides brief
descriptions of the amendments. Also emphasized is James Madison's role in
drafting and promoting the Bill of Rights.

Link to this Internet site from http://www.myreportlinks.com

▶**The American Presidency: James Madison**
This Web site offers a biography of James Madison. Here you will learn about
his early life, his role in the drafting of the Constitution, his opposition to the
Federalists, and his years as secretary of state and president.

Link to this Internet site from http://www.myreportlinks.com

▶**American Presidents: Life Portraits—James Madison**
At this Web site you will find "Life Facts" and "Did you know?" trivia about
James Madison. You will also find a letter from Madison to his father
regarding his honeymoon, an image gallery, and his two inaugural addresses.

Link to this Internet site from http://www.myreportlinks.com

▶**The Burning of Washington**
During the War of 1812 the British set fire to the Capitol building in
Washington. This Web site tells the story of the attack and how American
soldiers retaliated.

Link to this Internet site from http://www.myreportlinks.com

▶**The Cabildo: The Battle of New Orleans**
Here you will find an article about the Battle of New Orleans illustrated by
paintings and other remnants from the war. You will also learn about key
players in the conflict, preparations for war, and about the battles.

Link to this Internet site from http://www.myreportlinks.com

▶**The Charters of Freedom**
The Charters of Freedom Web site provides brief biographies of all delegates
to the Constitutional Convention, including James Madison. You will also
find the Bill of Rights and other amendments made to the Constitution.

Link to this Internet site from http://www.myreportlinks.com

Report Links

The Internet sites described below can be accessed at
http://www.myreportlinks.com

▶ **The Debates in the Federal Convention
of 1787 by James Madison**
Here you will find the complete set of notes taken by James Madison
on the debates of the 1787 Constitutional Convention in Philadelphia.
Madison's notes appear in the original form with helpful footnotes from
the editor.   Link to this Internet site from http://www.myreportlinks.com

▶ **Dolley Madison Project**
The Dolley Madison Project provides biographical material, personal
correspondence, time lines and images.

Link to this Internet site from http://www.myreportlinks.com

▶ *Federalist Papers* **Authored by James Madison**
At the Founding Fathers info Web site, you will find *The Federalist
Papers* written by James Madison and others. Also included are links to
the "The Constitution," "Bill of Rights," "The Anti-Federalist Papers,"
and other important documents of the time.

Link to this Internet site from http://www.myreportlinks.com

▶ **The Founders' Constitution**
Here you will find the complete text of the Constitution of the United
States of America, Bill of Rights, Declaration of Independence, and
other related documents, speeches, essays, and letters.

Link to this Internet site from http://www.myreportlinks.com

▶ **Founding Father**
Here you will find a discussion honoring James Madison's two-hundred
and fiftieth birthday. The participants include United States Supreme
Court Chief Justice William Rehnquist, among others.

Link to this Internet site from http://www.myreportlinks.com

▶ **"I Do Solemnly Swear . . ."**
Experience James Madison's first inauguration on March 4, 1809.
Included at this Web site are images and the text to Madison's
inaugural address.

Link to this Internet site from http://www.myreportlinks.com

 The Internet sites described below can be accessed at
http://www.myreportlinks.com

▶ **The Louisiana Purchase Exhibit**
This in-depth history of the Louisiana Purchase covers the negotiations,
debate over the constitutionality of the purchase, and the governing of the
area. Biographies and portraits of key players, as well as a number of maps
from 1565 to 1853, can also be found here.

Link to this Internet site from http://www.myreportlinks.com

▶ **Montpelier: The Home of James Madison**
At Montpelier, the home of James Madison, you will find Madison's
biographical information, Montpelier history, visitor information, and more.

Link to this Internet site from http://www.myreportlinks.com

▶ **Monroe Doctrine**
Within this article you will find the story of the "Monroe Doctrine," from
the circumstances which prompted an official United States stance on
European intervention in the Western Hemisphere to the policy's evolution.

Link to this Internet site from http://www.myreportlinks.com

▶ **Objects from the Presidency**
By navigating through this site you will find objects related to all the
United States presidents, including James Madison. You can also read a
brief description of Madison, the era he lived in, and learn about the
office of the presidency.

Link to this Internet site from http://www.myreportlinks.com

▶ **On These Walls**
Visit the James Madison Memorial and Museum which opened in 1980. Also
available on the Web site are the ten inscriptions from James Madison's writings.

Link to this Internet site from http://www.myreportlinks.com

▶ **"Peace Upon Honorable Terms"**
On February 16, 1815, President Madison approved the Treaty of Ghent. This
comprehensive article discusses the reasons for the United States declaration of
war with Britain, the events of the war, the negotiation process, and how the
treaty is viewed historically.

Link to this Internet site from http://www.myreportlinks.com

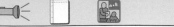
Report Links

The Internet sites described below can be accessed at
http://www.myreportlinks.com

▶ **President James Madison Approved an Act of Congress to Purchase Thomas Jefferson's Library**
America's Story from America's Library, a Library of Congress Web site, tells the story of when Madison passed an act of Congress to buy Thomas Jefferson's library.

Link to this Internet site from http://www.myreportlinks.com

▶ **"Star-Spangled Banner" and the War of 1812**
The Smithsonian Web site tells the story of how the 1814 British bombardment at Fort McHenry and the United States flag inspired the poem, and eventual national anthem, "The Star-Spangled Banner."

Link to this Internet site from http://www.myreportlinks.com

▶ **The War of 1812 Web Site**
This comprehensive Web site about the War of 1812 holds war diaries, battle descriptions, diagrams of British regiments, biographies, and much more.

Link to this Internet site from http://www.myreportlinks.com

▶ **The White House: Dolley Payne Todd Madison**
The official White House Web site holds the biography of First Lady Dolley Payne Todd Madison. Here you will learn about her early life, her marriage to Madison, and her years as first lady.

Link to this Internet site from http://www.myreportlinks.com

▶ **The White House: James Madison**
The official White House Web site holds the biography of James Madison. Here you will learn about Madison's life, presidency, and contributions to the United States Constitution.

Link to this Internet site from http://www.myreportlinks.com

▶ ***World Almanac for Kids Online*: James Madison**
The *World Almanac for Kids Online* provides essential information about James Madison. Here you will learn about the Constitutional Convention and other events related to his presidency.

Link to this Internet site from http://www.myreportlinks.com

Highlights

1751—*March 16:* James Madison is born on his grandfather's plantation on the Rappahannock River, in Port Conway, Virginia.

1760—Madison family moves to family home in Montpelier, Orange County, Virginia.

1762—Enrolled at boarding school of Donald Robertson for five years.

1769—*July:* Enrolls at the College of New Jersey, later renamed Princeton University.

1771—*Sept.:* Graduates from the College of New Jersey.

1776—Elected delegate to the Virginia Convention.

1779—Elected delegate to the Continental Congress in Philadelphia.

1781—Proposes amendment to Articles of Confederation.

1787—Madison, Alexander Hamilton, and John Jay begin publication of *The Federalist Papers.*

—Serves as delegate to the Constitutional Convention; proposes new constitution for the United States government.

1789—Elected to the House of Representatives of the First Federal Congress.

—Drafts Bill of Rights.

1794—*Sept. 15:* Marries Dolley Payne Todd.

1801—Becomes secretary of state under Thomas Jefferson.

1803—Is influential in Jefferson's decision to make the Louisiana Purchase.

1809—*March 4:* Sworn in as fourth president of the United States.

1812—*June 18:* Signs declaration of war against Great Britain commencing the War of 1812.

1814—*Aug. 24:* British troops capture and burn Washington, D.C.

1815—*Dec. 24:* Treaty of Ghent signed.

—*Jan. 8:* Andrew Jackson defeats British at Battle of New Orleans.

1817—Retires to Montpelier.

1829—Participates in the Virginia Constitutional Convention.

1836—*June 28:* Dies at Montpelier.

Dinner at the White House, 1814

It was after 9:00 P.M. on August 24, 1814, and the White House was deserted. Two men, General Robert Ross, commander of four thousand British troops, and Rear Admiral Sir George Cockburn, leader of the invading British fleet in Chesapeake Bay outside Maryland, entered the White House dining room. They then sat down to the dinner that had been prepared hours before for the fourth president of the United States, James Madison. At the other end of

▲ In August 1814, British troops marched into Washington, D.C., and set fire to the White House, burning it down. Fortunately, President James Madison and his wife, Dolley, were able to escape in time.

Pennsylvania Avenue, the Capitol, which had been set on fire by the British, was burning. As they ate their dinner, Cockburn mockingly drank a toast to "Jemmy's [the president's] health."[1]

The president and Mrs. Madison had fled from Washington as the British troops approached the city. After they finished dinner, Cockburn ordered fires set in each of the windows of the White House. It was burned to the ground. The only government building left unburned was the Patent Office.

First Lady Dolley Madison had left the White House at 3:00 P.M., before the British arrived. She had assured Madison she would make certain "Cabinet papers, public and private," were safe from destruction.[2] The first lady also managed to save the White House silver, some curtains, and the portrait of George Washington. Earlier that day, James Madison had ridden off on horseback with Attorney General Richard Rush across the Potomac River. He met up with Dolley the next day and they returned to Washington on August 27. Since the White House was destroyed, the president and the first lady stayed with friends.

This episode was the lowest point for America in the War of 1812 between the United States and Great Britain.

Boyhood, 1751–1767

James Madison was born on March 16, 1751, at his grandmother's house in Port Conway in the western part of Virginia. Within ten days, Madison was taken to his father's house in Orange County, Virginia, at the foot of the Blue Ridge Mountains. Madison's great-great-grandfather, John Madison, had arrived in Virginia from

▲ Montpelier served as a home for three generations of Madisons, including James Madison, Jr. Although he lived there almost all of his life, he did not inherit the estate until 1801 at the age of fifty.

England in 1652. By the time James Madison was born, the family was well established in the area. Madison's father, James Madison, Sr., owned nearly four thousand acres, on part of which he grew tobacco with the aid of slaves. His mother, Eleanor Conway Madison, was the daughter of a well-known planter and tobacco producer. One of Madison's boyhood memories was helping move furniture into the new house, Montpelier, when he was about nine years old.[1] Montpelier would remain Madison's home for the rest of his life.

Frances Madison, James's grandmother, widowed at thirty-two, was a strong independent woman. She raised her children and managed the plantation with the help of twenty-nine slaves. Tobacco, the main crop grown on the plantation, was exported to England. Most of what was needed on the plantation was then imported from England. Madison's grandmother lived with his family, and it was she who taught young James until her death in 1762. He may have also been educated by schoolmasters who instructed local children.

In June 1763, James was sent to a boarding school founded by Donald Robertson. There, he studied English, Latin, Greek, geometry, and algebra. Robertson, a graduate of the University of Edinburgh in Scotland, was a great influence on James. Madison later remarked, "all that I have been in life I owe largely to that man."[2] He stayed at Robertson's school for five years. Then, he received two years of private education at Montpelier by Anglican minister Thomas Martin, a graduate of the College of New Jersey in Princeton, New Jersey. Today, this school is known as Princeton University.

Chapter 3 ▶

Collegian to Secretary of State, 1769–1809

Madison, accompanied by Martin, Martin's brother Alexander, and a slave named Sawney set off in June 1769, for Princeton, New Jersey. Madison had decided to enroll at the College of New Jersey. The three hundred-mile trip on horseback took Madison through Virginia and Pennsylvania, then still colonies in the British Empire.

At the college, Madison studied Greek and Latin, mathematics, and philosophy. He began the study of government with a course called the "Law of Nature and of Nations." Madison lived at one of the student halls and ate his meals in the school dining room. Although he came from a wealthy family, Madison still had to watch how much he spent. In one letter to his father, Madison promised to keep his expenses down, as his father had requested.[1]

Madison graduated from the College of New Jersey in September 1771, but he stayed at the college until April 1772. During this time, he briefly studied law and Hebrew. When he returned to Montpelier, Madison began tutoring his younger brother and sisters. While Madison still had no idea of his future plans, he was already thinking about public debates, particularly on the subject of religious freedom. The Anglican Church was the established religion of Virginia, supported by taxes of Virginia citizens. Six Baptists had been jailed in Virginia for writing about their religious beliefs. Madison wrote to a friend about the imprisonment, "I have squabbled and scolded, abused and ridiculed so long about it, to so little purposes that I am

without common patience. So . . . I leave you to pity me and pray for liberty of conscience to revive among us."[2]

▶ Revolution

Madison strongly supported the colonies' resistance to the British government's efforts to impose its authority on the thirteen colonies. As early as August 1774, he supported defensive measures against the British.[3] In October 1775, Madison was appointed colonel of the militia for Orange County by the Virginia committee of safety. His father was his superior officer. In April 1776, Madison was elected a delegate to the Virginia Convention, a meeting that would help to decide the question of independence from Great Britain. On May 15, 1776, the Virginia Convention resolved unanimously to instruct its delegates to attend the Second Continental Congress in Philadelphia, to declare the thirteen colonies "free and independent states."[4] The Declaration of Independence was adopted on July 4, 1776. Madison spent the next four years of the Revolutionary War in Virginia developing the state government in partnership with Thomas Jefferson. In March 1780, at the age of twenty-nine, Madison served as one of Virginia's seven delegates to the Continental Congress in Philadelphia. He served in the Continental Congress for almost four years, not returning to Montpelier until the peace treaty with Britain was signed in 1783.

▶ Articles of Confederation

Until March 1781, the United States Congress operated under no formal agreement of government. There was no constitution, or document outlining the powers of Congress. It was only the agreement of the thirteen colonies, through their representatives in Congress, that permitted the Revolutionary War to be fought. As early as July 1776, the "Articles of Confederation and Perpetual Union" had been drafted to provide a unified government for the thirteen colonies, now thirteen independent states.

The Articles of Confederation was argued and debated until November 1777, when it was adopted by Congress. Then, the sates had to ratify the document. The Articles became effective in March 1781, when Maryland finally ratified. While the Articles created a weak central government, the powers of the individual states remained far greater. There was no federal head of government and no federal court system. Since money came from the states, Congress had no way to get money on its own, except what it might obtain from sale of the western lands.

Winning the Revolutionary War and settling the claims of the states to the western lands were the two major successes of Congress under the Articles. From the beginning, Madison realized the weakness of the national

▲ *James Madison is often referred to as "the Father of the Constitution" because of his active role in its creation and ratification.*

government under the Articles. Twelve days after they were ratified, Madison proposed an amendment to the Articles to give the United States government "a general and implied power" to act against any state that refused to obey the laws of Congress.[5]

Matters grew worse as the war came to a close. There was no national currency. Instead, states printed their own money, which soon became worthless. Farmers were ruined by debt, and manufacturers were ruined by each state setting its own import tax.

▶ Constitutional Convention

On May 25, 1787, in Philadelphia, a convention met to discuss amending the Articles of Confederation. Congress had asked the states to send delegates to a convention in Philadelphia "for the sole and express purpose of revising the Articles of Confederation."[6] George Washington was elected president of the convention. Madison was one of Virginia's delegates to the convention. The convention's meetings and debates were held in secret. Madison made careful notes of the debates and proceedings of the convention. It is those notes that remain the most complete record of the creation of the Constitution.[7]

Madison also drafted the proposals known as the "Virginia Plan," which formed the basis of the convention's debates.[8] Madison's proposals called for a totally new government to replace the existing government. The convention abandoned the idea of amending the Articles of Confederation and voted to establish a national government consisting of a supreme legislative, executive, and judiciary.[9] / separation of powers

The convention continued to meet for four months, at the end of which on September 28, 1787, Congress submitted the new Constitution to the states for ratification. The last article of the new Constitution required ratification by nine states before it became effective.

► The Federalist Papers

Immediately after the Constitution was submitted to the states for ratification, groups formed throughout the country opposing or supporting ratification. The group that supported ratification and a strong national government was known as the Federalists.[10] Washington, Madison, Alexander Hamilton, and John Jay were among its leading

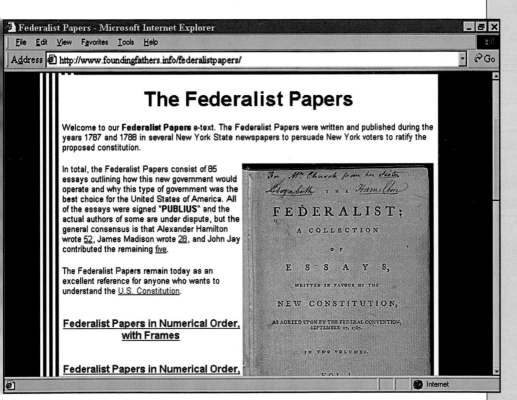

▲ James Madison was a prominent member of the Federalist Party, which strongly supported the ratification of the Constitution. Together, he, John Jay, and Alexander Hamilton published eighty-five articles known as The Federalist Papers, arguing in favor of the new Constitution's passage.

members. The group that opposed ratification of the Constitution and a strong national government was called the Anti-Federalists. Its prominent members included Patrick Henry, George Clinton, Sam Adams, Henry Lee, and George Mason. The Anti-Federalists opposed ratification on the grounds that the Constitution provided a federal government that could become too big and powerful. The Anti-Federalists' main argument was that a group could gain a majority in the national government and destroy the people's freedom for which the Revolutionary War had been fought. Madison, Jay, and Hamilton, under the name "Publius," published eighty-five articles in 1787 and 1788, arguing for ratification of the new Constitution. The collected articles are now known as *The Federalist* or *The Federalist Papers.* In "No. 10," one of his most famous essays, Madison argued against fears that the Constitution would allow the majority to tyrannize the minority. His argument was that the size of the United States and the huge variety of interests throughout the country would prevent "any one party from being able to outnumber and oppress the rest."[11]

Ratification of the Constitution was fairly swift. By June 21, 1788, New Hampshire became the ninth state to ratify. March 9, 1789, was the date set for the meeting of the new Congress in New York City, which was chosen as the temporary United States capital. The new government would represent a population of 4 million living in an area that extended from the Atlantic Ocean to the Mississippi River, though most people lived east of the Appalachian Mountains. In elections for the new government, George Washington was unanimously elected president, and John Adams vice president. Madison was elected to the House of Representatives, which Madison preferred to serve in, rather than the Senate.[12] Thomas Jefferson was appointed secretary of state and Alexander Hamilton became secretary of the treasury.

▶ The Bill of Rights

A principal argument against ratification of the Constitution was that it contained no mention of specific rights of the individual to certain freedoms, such as freedom of speech and religion. Ratification succeeded partly because it was agreed that after ratification, amendments to the Constitution would be enacted by Congress listing certain rights of the people.[13] Madison prepared the drafts of the proposed amendments. *First* Ten amendments to the Constitution, collectively known as the "Bill of Rights," were finally adopted. The ten amendments basically recognized things such as freedom of religion, speech, the press, assembly, and petition, among others.[14]

Madison had worked closely with Alexander Hamilton in promoting a strong central government but broke with him over whether the federal government should pay off the states' debts. Madison had

Alexander Hamilton and James Madison both supported a strong federal government. However, Madison believed that a strict interpretation of the Constitution was necessary to ensure protection of states' rights.

first worked with Thomas Jefferson in Virginia when Madison was a delegate to the Virginia Assembly. Even though he was secretary of state in Washington's administration, Jefferson fought against what he perceived as the increasing power of the federal government. Jefferson and Madison believed that if the federal government paid the states' debts, it would greatly increase the power of the federal government. They finally agreed to allow the federal government to assume the debt in exchange for Hamilton's support in moving the nation's capital to what would become Washington, D.C.

The conflict over the powers of the federal government led to the growth of factions, which eventually led to political parties. Hamilton and his followers were believers in a strong central federal government with broad interpretation of the government's power under the Constitution. Madison and Jefferson believed in a federal government with strict interpretation of the Constitution to limit its powers.[15] Hamilton and his followers called themselves "Federalists." In 1791, Madison referred to his group as the "Republican Party."[16] It soon became known as the Democratic-Republican Party.

▶ Dolley Madison

Until now Madison had lived in boardinghouses in Washington, without a wife or family. His life was about to change.

James Madison was forty-three years old when he met twenty-six-year old Dolley Payne Todd, a widow with two children, in 1794. Dolley, who was a Quaker, was well known in Washington. Her sister was married to George Washington's nephew, and Aaron Burr was one of

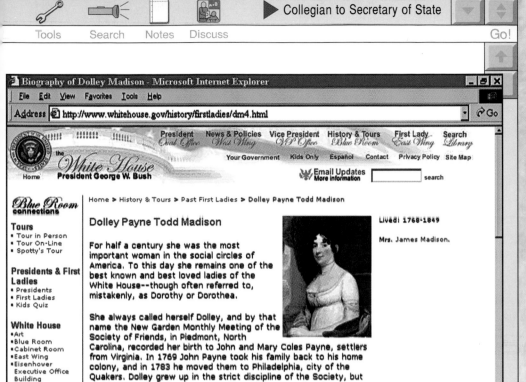

Biography of Dolley Madison - Microsoft Internet Explorer

File   Edit   View   Favorites   Tools   Help

Address http://www.whitehouse.gov/history/firstladies/dm4.html

President   News & Policies   Vice President   History & Tours   First Lady   Search
Oval Office   West Wing   VP Office   Blue Room   East Wing   Library

Your Government   Kids Only   Español   Contact   Privacy Policy   Site Map

the White House
President George W. Bush

Email Updates
More information   search

Home
Blue Room
connections

Home ➤ History & Tours ➤ Past First Ladies ➤ Dolley Payne Todd Madison

Tours
- Tour in Person
- Tour On-Line
- Spotty's Tour

Presidents & First Ladies
- Presidents
- First Ladies
- Kids Quiz

White House
- Art
- Blue Room
- Cabinet Room
- East Wing
- Eisenhower Executive Office Building
- Facts
- Oval Office
- Room Descriptions
- Vice President's Office
- West Wing

Dolley Payne Todd Madison

Lived: 1768-1849

Mrs. James Madison.

For half a century she was the most important woman in the social circles of America. To this day she remains one of the best known and best loved ladies of the White House--though often referred to, mistakenly, as Dorothy or Dorothea.

She always called herself Dolley, and by that name the New Garden Monthly Meeting of the Society of Friends, in Piedmont, North Carolina, recorded her birth to John and Mary Coles Payne, settlers from Virginia. In 1769 John Payne took his family back to his home colony, and in 1783 he moved them to Philadelphia, city of the Quakers. Dolley grew up in the strict discipline of the Society, but nothing muted her happy personality and her warm heart.

RELATED Whitehouse.gov Links

John Todd, Jr., a lawyer, exchanged marriage vows with Dolley in 1790. Just three years later he died in a yellow-

Internet

▲ *Aside from her charming personality and social graces, Dolley Madison will forever be famous for saving the portrait of George Washington from the burning White House in August 1814.*

her closest friends and advisors. In May 1794, Burr wrote to Dolley that Madison had asked to see her that evening.[17]

Dolley Todd's grandfather had fled persecution against Quakers in Great Britain to settle in Virginia as a farmer. Dolley's parents, Mary and John Payne, were devoted Quakers who moved first to North Carolina then to a farm in Virginia. Dolley was educated with her brothers at the local schoolhouse. This was unusual, because most girls did not receive an education at that time. As a plantation owner, Dolley's father owned slaves—but slavery was becoming unacceptable to most Quakers.

As early as 1778, the Quaker Meeting House that Dolley's parents belonged to had bought a book in which to record each slave freed by its members.[18] Mary and John Payne were assigned the task of keeping the book. However, it was not until 1782 that Virginia permitted an owner to free his slaves. Within a year, Payne had freed his slaves and moved the family to Philadelphia. Payne did not succeed as a businessman and by 1789, was disfellow-shipped by his Quaker Meeting House for not being able to pay his dues. He died three years later. John Todd, Jr., a Quaker and lawyer, had been courting Dolley since 1786. They were married on January 7, 1790. Their marriage was happy but short. John Todd died in a yellow fever epidemic that broke out in Philadelphia in August 1793. Dolley was left a widow with a son, John Payne Todd. Another son, William Temple Todd, died in infancy.

Dolley was not Madison's first love. He had fallen in love in 1782, at the age of thirty-one with Catherine "Kitty" Floyd, who was fifteen at the time. By April 1783, Madison and Kitty were engaged; however, by August, Kitty had left Madison and married a doctor named William Clarkson. Thomas Jefferson wrote to comfort Madison: "I sincerely lament the misadventure which has happened, from whatever cause it may have happened."[19]

Friends of Dolley and Madison encouraged them to marry, including Martha Washington who advised Dolley that Madison would make her ". . . a good husband and [that he was] all the better for being so much older."[20] James Madison and Dolley Payne Todd were married on September 15, 1794, at Harewood, the home of Washington's nephew and his wife, Dolley's sister. Not everyone supported Dolley's marriage to Madison. On December 12, 1794, Dolley was disfellowshipped by the

Thomas Jefferson was a ▶ personal friend and political ally of James Madison.

Quakers for marrying a non-Quaker.[21]

▶ Madison and Jefferson

Madison continued to serve in Congress through Washington's two terms in office. Washington was succeeded by John Adams, the second president of the United States. Madison insisted on retiring at the end of Washington's term and even refused an offer from the Virginia Assembly for election as governor of that state.[22] Madison returned to Montpelier, where for the next four years, he managed the plantation. During this time, he kept up an active correspondence with Thomas Jefferson, who was elected vice president for the Adams administration. At that time, candidates from different parties were often elected to the office of vice president and president.

Jefferson opposed Adams's attempts to increase the powers of the federal government. Madison was a strong supporter of Jefferson, particularly in Jefferson's fight against Adams's Alien and Sedition Acts. The acts threatened any citizen for "false and malicious" writings against the government and its officials. Any foreigner the government

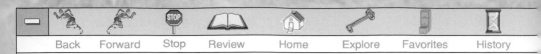
considered dangerous could be deported immediately. To oppose the acts, Madison drafted the Virginia Resolution and Jefferson drafted the Kentucky Resolution, which declared the Alien and Sedition Acts unconstitutional. The resolutions promoted the idea that the Union was an agreement or "compact" among the states, which gave each state the right to impose their views on the federal government. The Kentucky Resolution went further and declared that the states had a right to nullify any act of the federal government the states considered unconstitutional.[23] Supporters of nullification claimed that the Constitution was a contract among each of the states that could be terminated if the terms of the contract were violated. Madison and opponents of nullification argued that all the states had entered into the Constitution, and therefore it could not be altered by any state individually.[24] The Alien and Sedition Acts lapsed in 1800, and were not renewed.

Secretary of State, 1801–1809

The election of 1800 resulted in a tie between Thomas Jefferson and Aaron Burr for the presidency. The House of Representatives had to decide the outcome, and elected Thomas Jefferson. On March 5, 1801, Jefferson submitted Madison's nomination as secretary of state, and it was quickly confirmed by the Senate. Madison's bout with an illness much like the disease epilepsy and his father's death prevented him from arriving in Washington until the following May. Madison would remain secretary of state for the next eight years.

▶ The Louisiana Purchase

The most dangerous threat to the United States at the beginning of Madison's term as secretary of state lay to the west of the United States in the Louisiana Territory. Navigation of the Mississippi River and the Port of New Orleans in Louisiana were essential to the commerce of the United States. In 1801, Spain ceded the territory of Louisiana to France. The powerful French, under the rule of Napoléon Bonaparte, controlled the Mississippi and New Orleans. This posed a direct threat to the United States. At first, Napoléon had ideas of building a great empire in Louisiana. However, Napoléon's thoughts changed when he was defeated in his attempt to reconquer Haiti from the slaves who had rebelled and gained their independence. Napoléon needed money for the war with Great Britain that would break out in May 1803. He also

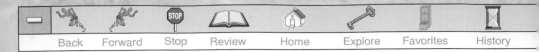

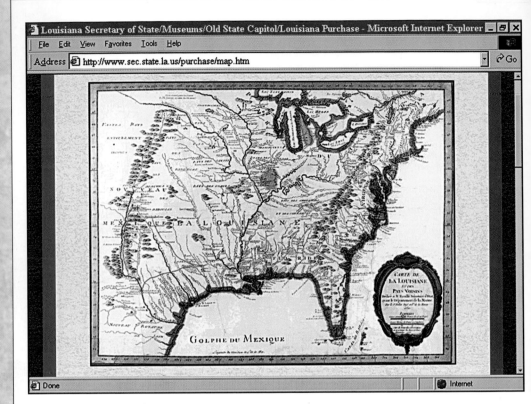

▲ The United States purchased from France all of the land extending from Canada to the Gulf of Mexico and from the Mississippi River to the Rocky Mountains for $15 million. This comes out to 4 cents per acre.

reasoned France could not hold onto Louisiana during the war with Great Britain. Napoléon offered to sell the Louisiana Territory, a total of 828,000 square miles for $15 million. Madison and Jefferson were astounded by the offer—they had been prepared to offer up to $9,375,000 for only New Orleans and parts of Florida.[1]

Madison and Jefferson had a problem with the purchase of the Louisiana Territory. Madison and Jefferson had always insisted on strict interpretation of the Constitution. They felt that any act of the government that

was not specifically included in the Constitution was unconstitutional, and therefore illegal. Opponents of the purchase maintained that the purchase of Louisiana was not expressly authorized by the Constitution. Jefferson believed that an amendment to the Constitution was necessary to permit the purchase. Madison reasoned that no amendment to the Constitution was necessary. In this case, Madison believed the benefits of the Louisiana Purchase to the nation were so great that a broader interpretation of the Constitution could be permitted.[2] Jefferson purchased the land for the United States on May 2, 1803. The Louisiana Territory, out of which thirteen states were carved, doubled the size of the United States, and led to its eventual expansion to the Pacific Ocean.

▶ Mediterranean Piracy

During the remainder of his term as secretary of state, Madison was mainly involved with the rights of the United States overseas. A major issue was piracy in the Mediterranean Sea, located between Europe and the northern coast of Africa. For years, ships from Morocco, Tripoli, Algeria, and Tunisia had taken American ships and sailors prisoner and held them for ransom. First the British, and later the American governments, paid tribute to the governments of those states to prevent attacks on their ships. The piracy in the Mediterranean continued until 1816, by which time ships of the United States Navy had defeated Algeria and Tunisia.

▶ British and French Attacks on American Shipping and Trade

Far more threatening to the United States than piracy in the Mediterranean was that Great Britain and France were now

Back   Forward   Stop   Review   Home   Explore   Favorites   History

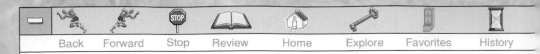

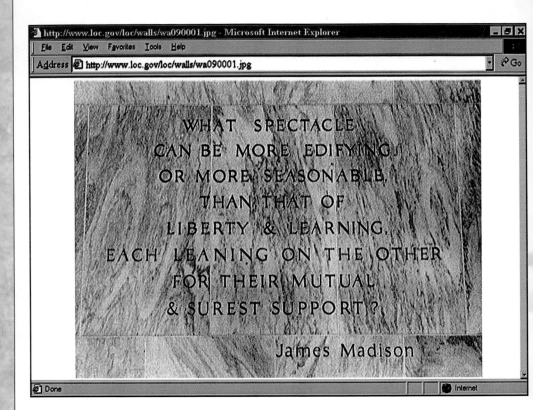

http://www.loc.gov/loc/walls/wa090001.jpg - Microsoft Internet Explorer

File Edit View Favorites Tools Help

Address http://www.loc.gov/loc/walls/wa090001.jpg   Go

WHAT SPECTACLE
CAN BE MORE EDIFYING,
OR MORE SEASONABLE,
THAN THAT OF
LIBERTY & LEARNING,
EACH LEANING ON THE OTHER
FOR THEIR MUTUAL
& SUREST SUPPORT?

James Madison

▲ *This quote by James Madison is inscribed on the entrance to the Madison Building. It is representative of his belief that knowledge is the key to individual liberty and democratic government.*

at war with each other. Britain and France would attack ships belonging to countries not involved in the war, in order to try to hurt each other's economy. Throughout the remainder of Madison's term as secretary of state, he devoted much of his time to fighting British and French attacks on America's trade and shipping. Both countries ignored the rights of neutral America and attacked its ships.

Most serious for the Americans was the British policy of impressment, or seizing American sailors for service on British ships. Britain was also determined to drive American ships from trade between French and Spanish colonies in the Caribbean Sea. The British did not consider ships sailing from those colonies to France and Spain to be neutral. Americans tried to get around this by buying goods from the French and Spanish colonies, importing them into the United States, and then shipping them to Europe. Britain argued this was a continuous voyage of the goods and was therefore subject to seizure by the British. The British referred to the Rule of 1756, which provided that trade not permitted in peacetime was not permitted during war. In peacetime, direct trade by Americans with those colonies was not permitted. Madison argued that the rule was overturned by Britain's treaties and its own acts. These acts permitted British subjects to trade with those colonies as well as Britain's enemies.[3]

In 1806, Napoléon issued the Berlin Decree, which permitted the seizure of ships trading with Britain. France began seizing American ships in European ports. Britain, relying on the Rule of 1756 and Orders issued in council in 1807, declared any ship trading in a European port no longer neutral. America had few weapons to fight and a weak army and navy. Madison decided to retaliate by advising Jefferson to cut off all trade with Britain and France. To do this, the Embargo Act was passed by Congress on December 22, 1807. It did not work. Every loophole in the act was exploited by shippers. American exports went across the Canadian border. Ships left American ports before the act could be enforced. Boats docked in European harbors claimed they had been driven there by storms, then unloaded valuable cargoes. In 1808, six hundred ships sailed for Europe with the government's permission. The embargo particularly damaged the South, which relied on the British market for export of the South's cotton. It did little to hurt Britain or France.

▶ Election of 1808

The Democratic-Republicans nominated Madison as their candidate for president. The Federalists nominated Charles Cotesworth Pinckney. The election of 1808 was fought mainly on the issue of the embargo. The Republicans supported the embargo, whereas the Federalists opposed it. Due to the harassment American shippers faced from the French and British, the embargo gained popular support. With the exception of New England, the embargo was widely accepted throughout the United States. Madison won the election with 122 electoral votes from Vermont, New Jersey, Pennsylvania, New York, Maryland, North Carolina, and most of the South and West. Pinckney gained 47 electoral votes from New England, Delaware, and some districts in Maryland and North Carolina.[4] George Clinton, a former vice president under Thomas Jefferson, was elected to be Madison's vice president as well.

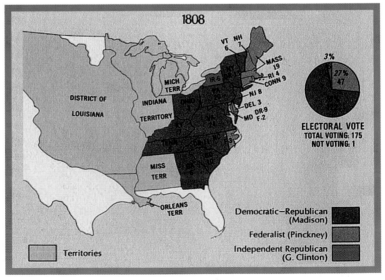

▲ Madison was the Democratic-Republican Party's candidate for president in the election of 1808. His overwhelming popularity was in part due to his support of the embargo.

Chapter 5 ▶

President of the United States, 1809–1817

James Madison was sworn in as president of the United States on March 4, 1809. Madison wore a plain suit made of American cloth. Dolley's gown was from Paris. A great ball was held in honor of the inauguration at which both the French and British ambassadors were present. Dolley redecorated the White House with $26,000 appropriated by Congress. Yet, behind the festivities was the far more serious threat of war. In his inaugural address, President Madison stressed the rights of America as a neutral nation in the ongoing dispute between France and Great Britain. He said, "It has been the true glory of the United States to cultivate peace by observing justice, and to entitle themselves to the respect of the nations at war by fulfilling their neutral obligations with the most scrupulous impartiality."

▶ War Threatens

Great Britain and France, the two most powerful nations in the Western world at that time, had been at war since 1803. Throughout this period, both countries' attacks on American trade increased. Each nation seized American ships and attempted to eliminate American trade with its enemy. The British continued their impressment of American sailors. Efforts at peace were under way, but the distance between London and Washington was too great. Before negotiations were complete, the United States decided to go to war.

▶ War of 1812

On June 1, 1812, Madison asked Congress for a declaration of war against Great Britain.

Madison cited four grounds: impressment of American sailors; violation of American neutrality; Britain's refusal to revoke orders banning neutral trade with France and her colonies; and the blockage of American ports by British ships.[1] War was declared on June 18, 1812.

The United States was ill prepared for war. Its army consisted of only 6,686 officers and infantry men. The army's major asset was 106 highly-trained officers from West Point. The army lacked a general staff for planning. Madison and Secretary of War John Armstrong plotted the strategy for war against the British. Although the American navy was tiny, it was experienced from its fights with the the pirates in the Mediterranean Sea. American strategy called for the conquest of Canada.[2] The navy would invade Canada from three directions—through Lake Champlain, along the Niagara River, and through Detroit. Except for Commodore Oliver H. Perry's victory on Lake Erie over the British navy, the invasions of Canada were failures.

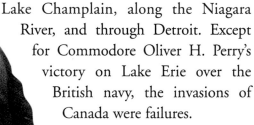

◀ Labeled "Mr. Madison's War" by political opponents, the War of 1812 loomed ahead as Madison was sworn in as the fourth president of the United States.

By 1814, the British had defeated Napoléon and were free to turn all their force on the Americans. The British attempted an invasion through Lake Champlain but were defeated by the American navy under Commodore Thomas Macdonough. Macdonough's victory ended any threat of a British invasion from Canada.[3]

The American navy's control of the Great Lakes ended the threat posed by the British and their American Indian allies. However, the Atlantic seacoast was blockaded by the British navy. The British raided towns and cities along the coast. Georgetown and Fredericktown in Maryland were two towns destroyed by the British navy.

▶ Washington Burns

In June 1814, the British sailed up Chesapeake Bay and landed at Benedict, Maryland. Washington, D.C., was located just forty miles away.

The British left Washington on August 25—the day after they burned it—and proceeded with the attack on Baltimore, Maryland. The Americans had about thirteen thousand men with another one thousand men defending Fort McHenry, located on an island in Baltimore Harbor. The American defenses at Baltimore were too strong for a British attack, but the British fleet was able to bombard Fort McHenry. The bombardment lasted forty-eight hours. Throughout the bombardment, a huge American flag remained flying from the fort. Watching from a British prison ship in the harbor, where he was trying to gain the release of an American, was Francis Scott Key. He was inspired by the sight of the flag still flying through all the mayhem. As the sun rose, he wrote "The Star-Spangled Banner."[4]

▶ Battle of New Orleans

The British war plans included the conquest of New Orleans, the chief port for America's exports from the West. The British fleet anchored in the Gulf of Mexico outside New Orleans and landed six thousand troops on the banks of the Mississippi River, just south of the city. General Andrew Jackson led approximately 3,500 men into battle. Jackson's forces included regular army units, militiamen, and white and black volunteers from New Orleans, including a French pirate named Jean Laffite. The battle began on January 8, 1815, and ended the same day. The British defeat was overwhelming with a loss of two thousand men killed or wounded and five hundred taken prisoner. Jackson's losses were seventy-one killed or wounded.[5]

News of the great victory at New Orleans arrived in Washington after the Treaty of Ghent between Great Britain and the United States had been signed on December 24, 1814. The United States and Great Britain had actually been negotiating peace since 1812. Britain insisted on border adjustments, removal of American warships on the Great Lakes, and an end to American fishing rights in Canadian waters. The United States demanded that the British end impressment, abandon the practice of blockades, and pay for the ships seized by the British. Both governments dropped their demands. The Treaty of Ghent simply restored the boundaries that existed prior to the war and settled a peace between the nations.[6]

▶ Remainder of Madison's Term

Madison was opposed in the presidential election of 1812 by a member of his own party, DeWitt Clinton. Although

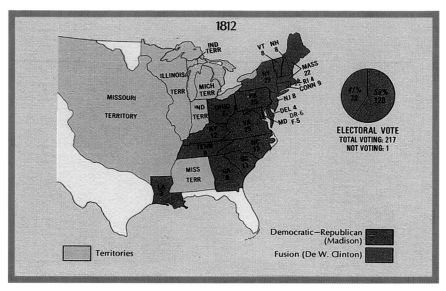

1812

IND.
TERR
VT 8   NH 8
ILLINOIS
TERR
MICH
TERR
MASS 22
NY 29
RI 4
CONN 9
MISSOURI
IND
TERR
OHIO 7
PA 25
NJ 8
TERRITORY
DEL 4
DR 6
MD F 5
KY 12
VA 25
TENN 8
NC 15
SC 11
MISS
TERR
GA 8
LA 3

ELECTORAL VOTE
TOTAL VOTING: 217
NOT VOTING: 1

Territories

Democratic–Republican
(Madison)

Fusion (De W. Clinton)

▲ Madison was reelected for a second administration in the election
of 1812.

he was a Republican, Clinton was supported by the
Federalists who were critical of Madison's conduct during
the war. Madison was reelected by 128 electoral votes to the
89 votes Clinton received. The electors who voted for the
president and vice president were appointed by the legislature in some states and elected by the people in other states.
Madison's first vice president, George Clinton, had died in
office on April 20, 1812. Elbridge Gerry of Massachusetts
was elected vice president for Madison's second term. Gerry
also died in office, on November 23, 1814.

The remainder of Madison's term was devoted to
domestic issues. Congress approved Madison's call for a
standing army, the first in America's history, and his efforts
to strengthen the navy. Since the White House was being
rebuilt, the Madisons moved into the buildings formerly
occupied by the Treasury Department, which First Lady

Dolley Madison redecorated. Madison was able to resume his visits to Montpelier. Since 1811, he had only been away from Washington a total of four months.

The three great issues dominating Madison's remainder of his term were tariffs, internal improvements (such as road building), and a national bank. All three issues involved Madison's belief in a strict interpretation of the Constitution, limiting the government's powers to act. Madison signed the bill creating the Second Bank of the United States despite the question of whether it was authorized by the Constitution. Madison said the question was decided by previous legislation and ". . . a concurrence of the general will of the nation."[7]

Madison also signed the bill for tariffs on foreign imports to support the growing manufacturers of the United States. However, although Madison believed it was necessary for the government to make improvements of roads and canals, he vetoed the bill for national improvements.

▲ The Treaty of Ghent was signed by the United States and Britain on December 24, 1814 in Ghent, Belgium. This provided peace between the two nations without resolving those issues that caused the war.

▲ *The Battle of New Orleans was fought in January 1815, before word that the treaty was signed could reach General Jackson.*

Supporters of the bill for national improvements argued that the government had implied powers under the Constitution to make the improvements. Madison replied that giving the government implied power to act would loosen "all the bonds of the Constitution."[8] Madison vetoed the bill on his last day as president, calling for an amendment to the Constitution to permit the government to make such improvements. Unless the Constitution was changed, Madison felt that internal improvements were the responsibility of the states.

Chapter 6

Retirement, 1817–1836

Packing up their belongings and attending numerous celebrations in honor of Madison delayed James and Dolley Madison's departure from Washington for over a month. Upon the inauguration of James Monroe, the fifth president, Madison retired to Montpelier. The Madisons

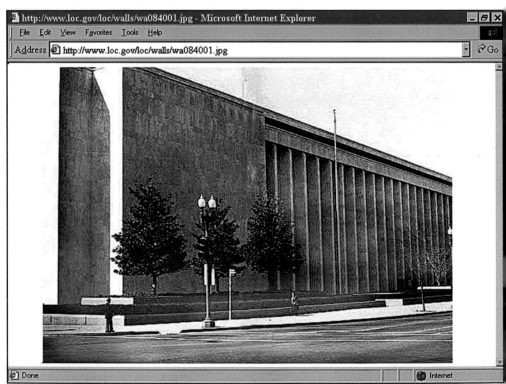

http://www.loc.gov/loc/walls/wa084001.jpg - Microsoft Internet Explorer

File   Edit   View   Favorites   Tools   Help

Address http://www.loc.gov/loc/walls/wa084001.jpg   Go

Done   Internet

▲ *The Madison Building, located in Washington, D.C., was opened in 1980 to pay homage to James Madison. It is the country's official memorial to the former president and part of the Library of Congress.*

arrived in Montpelier by steamboat and carriage. Madison never returned to Washington.

When Madison returned to Montpelier, he resumed his life as a plantation owner. He depended on the plantation for his income. The plantation mainly produced tobacco grown by slaves. Madison had switched from grain and wheat after peace between France and Great Britain reduced their demands for wheat and grain.

Throughout Madison's retirement, numerous people visited Montpelier, namely Thomas Jefferson and the Marquis de Lafayette who was on tour of America. Though retired, Madison remained active in national affairs. In 1823, almost all of Spain's colonies in South America had declared their independence from Spain. France and Russia threatened to help Spain reimpose her control over the South American republics. Great Britain offered to join the United States in a declaration against any European interference in South America. President James Monroe asked Madison and Jefferson for their advice. Madison urged Monroe to join Great Britain in the declaration against European intervention.[1] Monroe decided against joining Great Britain, and sided instead with Secretary of State John Quincy Adams. Monroe issued his own declaration, called the "Monroe Doctrine." The Monroe Doctrine declared that the American continents could no longer ". . . be considered as subjects for future colonization by a European power."[2]

Madison entered public life again in 1829 as a delegate to draft a new constitution for Virginia. His most important achievement at the convention was to extend the right to vote to every white male who paid taxes, instead of limiting the vote to landholders only. In 1831 and 1832, Madison again became involved in the issue of "nullification"

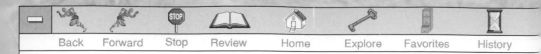
by which certain states claimed the right to "nullify" any law of the United States that they believed violated their rights.

One of these states was South Carolina, which suffered greatly from the affects of the tariff acts of 1828 and 1832. From 1832 to 1833, South Carolina called a state convention at which the tariff acts were declared null and void. The convention further provided that South Carolina would secede from the Union if the United States tried to enforce the tariff. Supporters of nullification quoted Jefferson's earlier writings, particularly the Kentucky Resolutions. Madison argued strongly in letters and newspaper articles against nullification. He maintained that questions of federal power and states' rights should be settled by the Supreme Court.[3] The threat of South Carolina's secession was overcome by President Jackson's threatened use of force and the lowering of tariffs.

Madison, together with Thomas Jefferson and James Monroe, met in July 1817 to lay the cornerstone for Central College, later known as the University of Virginia. Madison devoted himself to the university, raising money and fighting in the Virginia legislature for Virginia's support of the school. In February 1818, the Virginia legislature authorized the university. Madison continued his interest in the university for the rest of his life. Madison left the bulk of his library to the University of Virginia.

◀ *James Monroe was a close colleague and friend of Madison.*

▶ Death

Madison retired at the age of sixty-eight. Although he had suffered from problems with his liver throughout his life, he enjoyed good health until 1831. By 1831, Madison's bouts with rheumatism (an illness of the joints and muscles) prevented him from leaving Montpelier. Madison occupied himself with arranging his papers, which he wanted to be held by the U.S. Congress. After Madison's death, Dolley was determined to keep all of her husband's papers together for delivery to the nation. Twelve years following Madison's death, and after years of debate, Congress accepted delivery of all of the documents. Congress awarded Dolley $25,000 in trust to save her from the constant demands for money from her son, John Payne Todd.[4]

Though he was weak and bedridden, to visitors, Madison "remained . . . as bright as ever, his intelligence, recollections, discrimination, and philosophy all delightfully instructive."[5] While eating breakfast on June 28, 1836, Madison had difficulty swallowing. "His niece, Nelly Willis, asked "What is the matter, Uncle James?" "Nothing more than a change of mind, my dear," he replied. His head instantly dropped, and he ceased breathing as quietly as the snuff of a candle goes out."[6] He was buried in the family plot half a mile away from Montpelier.

James Madison's greatest contribution to the history of the United States was not as secretary of state or president of the United States. It was Madison's role in the drafting of the U.S. Constitution and its ratification, together with his role in drafting the Bill of Rights, for which he received recognition. In 1827, Madison was referred to as the "Father of the Constitution."[7] Madison's notes and records of the Constitutional Convention serve as the most complete record of the making of the United States Constitution.

Chapter Notes

Chapter 1. Dinner at the White House, 1814

1. Ralph Ketcham, *James Madison: A Biography* (Charlottesville: The University Press of Virginia, 1996), p. 579.

2. Ibid, p. 576.

Chapter 2. Boyhood, 1751–1767

1. Irving Brant, *The Fourth President: A Life of James Madison* (Indianapolis: The Bobbs-Merrill Company, 1970), p. 6.

2. Ralph Ketcham, *James Madison: A Biography* (Charlottesville: The University Press of Virginia, 1996), p. 21.

Chapter 3. Collegian to Secretary of State, 1769–1809

1. Irving Brant, *The Fourth President: A Life of James Madison* (Indianapolis: The Bobbs-Merrill Company, 1970), p. 11.

2. Ibid., p. 17.

3. Ibid., pp. 26–27.

4. Ralph Ketcham, *James Madison: A Biography* (Charlottesville: The University Press of Virginia, 1996), p. 70.

5. Ibid., p. 113.

6. George Brown Tindall and David E. Shi, *America: A Narrative History* (New York: W. W. Norton & Company, 1996), p. 300.

7. Frank Donovan, *Mr. Madison's Constitution* (New York: Dodd, Mead & Company, 1965), p. viii.

8. Tindall and Shi, p. 303.

9. Donovan, p. 45.

10. Alfred H. Kelly, Winfred A. Harbison, and Herman Belz, *The American Constitution: Its Origins & Development* (New York: W. W. Norton & Company, Inc., 1983), p. 107.

11. Benjamin F. Wright, ed., *The Federalist* (New York: Friedman/Fairfax, 1961), p. 135.

12. Brant, p. 223.

13. Tindall and Shi, p. 325.

14. Kelly, Harbison, and Betz, pp. 121–122.

15. Ibid., pp. 130–131.

16. Brant, p. 256.

17. Katherine Anthony, *Dolley Madison: Her Life and Times* (Garden City, N.Y.: The Country Life Press, 1949), p. 79.

18. Ibid., p. 14.

19. Ibid., p. 68.

20. Ibid., p. 83.

21. Ketcham, p. 381.

22. Ibid., p. 368.

23. Tindall and Shi, p. 355.

24. Ibid., p. 627.

Chapter 4. Secretary of State, 1801–1809

1. Irving Brant, *James Madison: Secretary of State 1800–1809* (Indianapolis: The Bobbs-Merrill Company, Inc., 1953), p. 109.

2. Ralph Ketcham, *James Madison: A Biography* (Charlottesville: University Press of Virginia, 1996), p. 422.

3. Brant, p. 298.

4. Ibid., p. 468.

Chapter 5. President of the United States, 1809–1817

1. Major James Ripley Jacobs and Glenn Tucker, *The War of 1812: A Compact History* (New York: Hawthorn Books, Inc., 1969), p. 12.

2. George Brown Tindall and David E. Shi, *America: A Narrative History* (New York: W. W. Norton & Company, 1996), p. 383.

3. Jacobs and Tucker, p. 156.

4. Ibid., pp. 151–152.

5. Ibid., p. 185.

6. Tindall and Shi, p. 390.

7. Ibid., p. 398.

8. Ralph Ketcham, *James Madison: A Biography* (Charlottesville: The University Press of Virginia, 1996), p. 610.

Chapter 6. Retirement, 1817–1836

1. Alexander De Conde, *A History of American Foreign Policy* (New York: Charles Scribner's Son, 1963), p. 138.

2. Ibid., p. 140.

3. Irving Brant, *The Fourth President: A Life of James Madison* (Indianapolis: The Bobbs-Merrill Company, 1970), p. 623.

4. Katherine Anthony, *Dolley Madison: Her Life and Times* (Garden City, N.Y.: The Country Life Press, 1949), p. 390.

5. Ralph Ketcham, *James Madison: A Biography* (Charlottesville: University Press of Virginia, 1996), p. 669.

6. Brant, p. 642.

7. Ibid., p. 197.

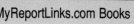
Gaines, Anne Graham. *James Madison: Our Fourth President.* Chanhassen, Minn.: The Child's World, Inc., 2001.

Hamilton, Alexander, James Madison, and John Jay. *The Federalist.* London: Phoenix Press, 2000.

Kelley, Brent P. *James Madison.* Broomall, Pa.: Chelsea House Publishers, 2001.

Kelly, Regina Z. *James Madison: Statesman and President.* Tarrytown, N.Y.: Marshall Cavendish Corporation, 1991.

Nardo, Don. *The American Revolution.* Farmington Hills, Mich.: Gale Group, 2002.

Pflueger, Lynda. *Dolley Madison: Courageous First Lady.* Berkeley Heights, N.J.: Enslow Publishers, Inc., 1999.

Santella, Andrew. *The War of 1812.* Danbury, Conn.: Children's Press, 2001.

Weber, Michael. *Madison, Monroe, and Quincy Adams.* Vero Beach, Fla.: Rourke Corporation, 1996.

Welsbacher, Anne. *James Madison.* Minneapolis: ABDO Publishing Company, 1998.

Wills, Garry, and Arthur Schlesinger, ed. *James Madison.* New York: Henry Holt & Company, 2002.

Index